The Children of
NEPAL

THE WORLD'S CHILDREN

The Children of
NEPAL

MATTI A. PITKÄNEN
WITH REIJO HÄRKÖNEN

Carolrhoda Books, Inc./Minneapolis

The publisher wishes to thank Anita Regmi and David Faust for their assistance with the preparation of this book.

This edition first published 1990 by Carolrhoda Books, Inc.
First published in Finland in 1985 by Otava Publishing Company Ltd.
under the title HIMALAJAN LAPSET.
Original edition copyright © 1985 by Matti A. Pitkänen
Additional text copyright © 1990 by Carolrhoda Books, Inc.

All English-language rights reserved by Carolrhoda Books, Inc.
No part of this book may be reproduced, stored in a retrieval system,
or transmitted in any form or by any means, electronic, mechanical,
photocopying, recording, or otherwise, without the prior written permission
of the Publisher except for the inclusion of brief quotations in an
acknowledged review.

Library of Congress Cataloging-in-Publication Data

Härkönen, Reijo.

  [Himalajan lapset. English]
  The children of Nepal / by Reijo Härkönen; photographs by Matti
A. Pitkänen.
     p.   cm. – (The World's children)
  Translation of: Himalajan lapset.
  Summary: An introduction to the history, geography, and people
of Nepal with emphasis on the day-to-day life of the children.
  ISBN 0-87614-395-8
  1. Nepal–Juvenile literature. 2. Children–Nepal–Juvenile
literature. [1. Nepal. 2. Nepal–Social life and customs.]
I. Pitkänen, Matti A., ill. II. Title. III. Series: World's
children (Minneapolis, Minn.)
DS493.4.H3513   1990
954.96–dc20   89-23923
                                                           CIP
                                                            AC

Manufactured in the United States of America

    2   3   4   5   6   7   8   9   10   99   98   97   96   95   94   93

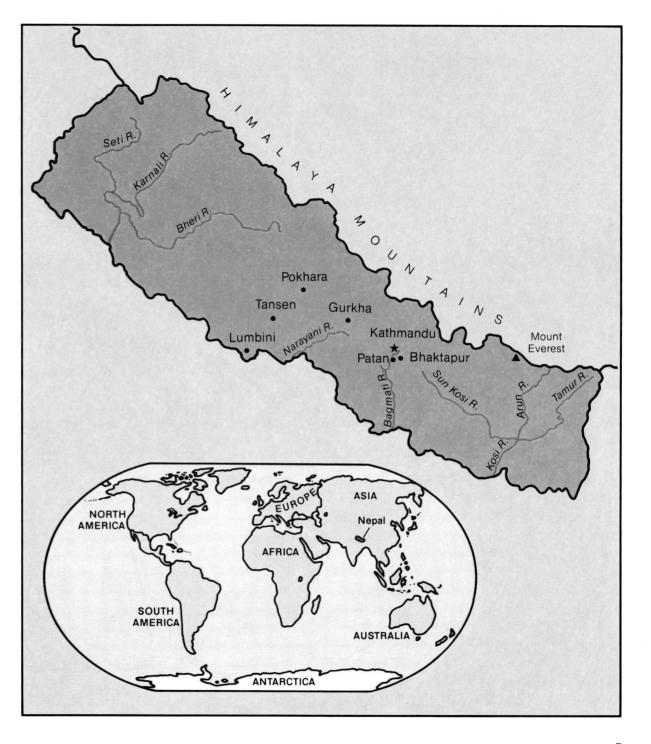

The morning's first rays of sunlight strike the world's highest peak, Mount Everest. The snowy slopes of the Himalaya Mountains turn blue, then red, as day breaks. The sun's rays move down the mountain slopes, passing over a herd of yaks lumbering through a pasture, touching on a mountain village, and finally reaching Nepal's waking capital city, Kathmandu, in the valley below.

The bells of Kathmandu's temples soon begin to ring, and early risers bring offerings of flowers and rice to the temples, asking the gods for luck for the day just begun.

In the jungle, a tiger returns from a successful overnight hunting trip and a crocodile slips silently from a muddy riverbank into the water. Nepal has awoken to a new day.

The land that is now Nepal was once several separate kingdoms, each with its own ruler. During the 1760s, one of the rulers, Prithvi Narayan Shah, took over the kingdoms surrounding his own. He named his new, larger land the Kingdom of Nepal.

The Shah family ruled Nepal until 1846, when the country's prime minister, Jung Bahadur, took the king's power away. Although the king remained on the throne, the prime minister actually ruled the country. Bahadur added the word *rana*, which means "royal," to his family's name.

During their reign, the Ranas closed Nepal to the outside world. It wasn't until 1951, when the Shah family overthrew the Ranas and regained their power, that outsiders were once more allowed to enter Nepal.

Because of its many years of isolation, Nepal is one of the least-developed countries in the world. While a few wealthy Nepalese have adopted the modern ways of other nations, change is slow to come. In most of Nepal, life continues much as it did decades, even centuries, ago.

Now that the sun is up, the first tradespeople have opened their shops on the roadsides of Kathmandu. A shop is often just a mat spread out on the ground. Some people sell fresh fruits and vegetables, such as lemons, tomatoes, eggplants, and garlic. Others offer bright-colored rugs or intricately carved statues. The best place to set up a shop is in front of a temple, where there are always plenty of people.

Togendra has come to the city to sell coconuts. He will give the money he earns to his parents to help support his family. Like most of the people of Nepal, Togendra's family does not have a lot of money.

It was before daybreak when Aani and two other women left their village to walk to the capital city, carrying heavy loads of wood on their backs. Now the wood has been sold, and the women are resting before making the three-hour journey home.

In Nepal, the more money a woman has, the more jewelry she wears. If a woman has no jewelry at all, she is probably very poor. These women are wearing nose rings, which is traditional for the Tamangs, the ethnic group to which they belong.

The Tamangs are one of the largest of Nepal's many ethnic groups. Each group has its own customs, which may be quite different from those of other ethnic groups. Although the official language of Nepal is Nepali, most groups even have their own language. In the past, Nepal's ethnic groups had very little contact with each other. This is changing, however, as methods of communication and transportation improve.

The city of Kathmandu and the surrounding valley have hundreds of Hindu and Buddhist temples. Religion is an important part of the daily lives of almost all of Nepal's people.

Hinduism was brought to Nepal centuries ago by immigrants from India, where the religion began. In modern times, most Nepalese are Hindu.

Pashupatinath, near Kathmandu, is one of Nepal's most famous Hindu temples. Pilgrims visit the temple from all parts of Nepal, most making the journey on foot. Baba is one of the holy men who lives within the temple area. He is very respected because he has set aside everyday cares to meditate and give advice about life and religion.

Sani and Hari take care of a small temple where people go to worship Ganesh, the Hindu god of learning. The two children keep the temple clean. The bells are rung when someone has a message for the elephant-headed god. The lions on either side of the steps keep peace in the temple.

Hindus believe God can appear in many different forms. The three most important forms are Brahma, the creator; Vishnu, the preserver; and Shiva, the destroyer. Each of these forms is also referred to as a god.

Hindus believe that the gods watch over them from birth until death. If the gods approve of them, then life will be good, but disaster may come from angering a god. People try to please the gods by bringing them such offerings as flowers, rice, coins, and even animals.

Bhairab is the god Shiva in his most terrible form. A many-armed black statue of Bhairab stands in the center of Kathmandu. It is said that anyone who tells a lie in front of this statue will die.

Most Nepalese who aren't Hindu are Buddhist. Nepal's Hindus and Buddhists have great respect for each other's religions. The two religions have existed peacefully together for so long in Nepal that they have begun to overlap. In fact, some Nepalese consider themselves to be both Hindu and Buddhist.

A *stupa* is a Buddhist temple. Swayambunath, with its beautiful gold-colored tower, is Nepal's oldest *stupa*. It is sometimes called the Monkey Temple because of the many monkeys that live on the offerings of food people leave there. The tower has the eyes of Buddha painted on each of its four sides.

Although Swayambunath is a Buddhist temple, there is a Hindu elephant statue in its courtyard. This mixture of the two religions is very common in Nepal, where the same temple is often used by both Buddhists and Hindus.

Buddha was a prince named Siddhartha Gautama, who was born in the town of Lumbini in what would one day be southern Nepal. The prince decided that the way to be happy was to treat others with respect and to live a simple, moral life of study. More than 2,500 years later, hundreds of millions of people still follow the teachings of the man who came to be called Buddha, which means Enlightened One.

In Nepal, all young boys who are Buddhists must enter a monastery, a place where monks live, for a short time. Some of them become monks and live in the monastery for the rest of their lives. Piyush, Ramesh, and Ashok are monks at the Bodhnath Stupa near Kathmandu. Buddhists consider it their duty to give monks gifts of food and money so that the holy men can spend their time meditating and studying Buddha's teachings.

A *thangka,* which is a colorful painting done on fabric, uses pictures to tell the story of Buddha's life. There are no words on a *thangka*. Because very few Nepalese can read, pictures and storytelling are still more common in Nepal than books and newspapers.

Six miles east of Kathmandu is the town of Bhaktapur. Rameshoweri and her family live in a house just outside of the town. Each morning, Rameshoweri's parents have a big breakfast before going to work in the fields. Rameshoweri takes care of her younger sister while her parents are working. After her parents have left, Rameshoweri uses her *patuka*, a wide strip of fabric, to tie her sister tightly to her back. Then she walks to Bhaktapur.

The temple is always Rameshoweri's first stop in town. Rameshoweri is a Hindu. It is her job to leave the family's offering of rice and flowers at the temple each morning.

After she has visited the temple, Rameshoweri spends the rest of the day wandering around Bhaktapur. Because she must take care of her sister, Rameshoweri does not go to school.

The main square is Rameshoweri's favorite place to visit in Bhaktapur. On the edge of the square is the Nyatapola Temple, Nepal's tallest temple. When she climbs to the top of the five-story building, Rameshoweri passes between the temple's statues. At the bottom of the stairs are two stone guards, followed by two elephants, two lions, two griffins—animals that are part lion and part eagle—and two goddesses. It is said that each pair of statues is more powerful than the one before.

From the top of the temple, Rameshoweri can look out over the square, which is usually filled with animals and people. Cows, considered holy by Hindus, roam freely through the streets and squares of the town. Tourists have discovered Bhaktapur, and with tourists come motorbikes and cars, cameras and gift shops. Sometimes Rameshoweri stops to talk to visitors to her town. She has even learned a few words of English.

The town of Bhaktapur looks very much as it did more than three hundred years ago when most of it was built by the Newars. Rameshoweri is a member of the Newar ethnic group. The Newars are skillful craftspeople, known especially for their elaborate wood carvings.

In the temples, there are carvings of gods and goddesses and imaginary beasts. Because glass was not yet known in Nepal at the time the temples were built, carvings of peacocks were sometimes used as windows. People can peek out between the gaps in the peacock's tail to see what is happening in the street below. The wooden feathers protect them from the wind.

About one hundred miles west of the Kathmandu valley, in the hills of central Nepal, is the town of Tansen. Like Rameshoweri, most of the people of Tansen are Newars.

Ananta is a musician who lives in Tansen. He plays the *saranghi,* a stringed instrument that looks like a violin. Because most Nepalese do not own a television or radio, they rely on musicians for entertainment. These important members of the community travel from place to place, playing at weddings, festivals, and anywhere else people gather to dance and sing.

Two women have stopped on the road to Tansen to talk. One of them is on her way to the market with a bagful of rice to sell. When the women first see each other, they say, "Have you eaten rice?" This is a common greeting in Nepal, where rice is one of the most important foods.

A typical meal in Nepal might include rice, vegetables seasoned with curry, and lentil soup. Most Nepalese can afford to eat only small amounts of meat and usually save it for special occasions. Hindus are forbidden to eat any beef at all.

Rame has lived in Tansen all of his life. Although he's only 14 years old, he has no time for school because he must go to work every day. Rame and his friend Kanchho are carriers. Their job is to carry loads from one place to another. Since there are few roads in Nepal, most goods must be transported by carriers or animals. It is hard work, and the days are long. The pay is not high, and what Rame does earn, he gives to his father.

Rame and Kanchho are each wearing a *topi,* the kind of hat worn by the men of Tansen. In Nepal, a hat may show where a person comes from, and it is considered bad luck to lose it.

There is no typical way to dress in Nepal. Every ethnic group has its own way of dressing. The men of one group wear baggy pants and Western-style jackets, while the men of another wear short skirts with blouses that tie in the front. Some women wear saris, which are long pieces of fabric wrapped into dresses. Other women wear long gowns with aprons.

When Nirmala was 16, she married a boy her parents had chosen for her when she was just a little girl. Now Nirmala is a parent herself.

Nirmala's little boy's name is Ramu. When Ramu was born, each of Nirmala's friends and neighbors gave him a few coins. Nirmala knows she must take good care of her son because so many of the children of Nepal die when they are very young.

Disease is common in Nepal, and there are few hospitals or doctors to treat people when they are sick. Nepal's government is working to reduce the number of deaths by vaccinating against certain diseases, providing clean water, and building hospitals.

Nirmala remembers her mother saying that if a baby cries a great deal, the child will marry someone who lives far away. Ramu is a quiet baby, so perhaps he will find a wife in his own village. Nirmala and her husband, like many young parents in Nepal, have decided to let Ramu choose his own wife.

The students at this school are taking a Sanskrit exam. The country's official language, Nepali, is based on Sanskrit, which is an ancient Indian language.

A Nepalese classroom is often just an open courtyard with no desks and few supplies. Many Nepalese children don't go to school. Sometimes the nearest school is too far away or has no teacher. Sometimes children have to help at home or work to earn money for the family. Boys go to school more often than girls do. Before the 1950s, most girls were forbidden to go to school at all.

Since then, Nepal's government has decided that all children deserve a good education. There are programs to build schools and train teachers, and every year more and more Nepalese learn how to read and write.

One of the jobs that keep Nepalese children too busy to go to school is farm work. About 9 out of 10 Nepalese are farmers. Most of Nepal's farmland lies in the southern and central parts of the country. Little can be grown in the mountainous north. The farm work is usually done by hand. Most families grow only enough food to feed themselves, and sometimes not even enough for that.

During the months from June through September, the monsoon winds bring almost nonstop rain to Nepal. Sometimes the rains are so heavy that they flood roads and wash fields into rivers. When the sky clears, it is time to harvest the crops.

A large variety of crops are grown in Nepal, including potatoes, wheat, corn, sugarcane, and many kinds of fruit. The most important crop, however, is rice. Rice is harvested with a *hasia,* or sickle. Most of the work is done by women and children. After the rice has been cut, it is threshed, which means the grains are separated from the stalks. The stalks, or straw, are then heaped into piles to be used as animal feed.

One of Nepal's most fertile farming regions is the Terai. The Terai is a flat strip of land on the southern border that runs from one end of Nepal to the other. It was once thick with mosquitoes that carried malaria, a deadly disease. During the 1950s and 1960s, the government sprayed the area with poison to kill the mosquitoes. Although there were still some of the dangerous insects left when they were through, the Terai was much safer than it had been. Many people moved into the area and began to farm the land.

One of the groups of people who lived in the Terai even before the attack on the mosquitoes was the Tharus. Most Tharus are farmers. They have their own language and their own traditions. A Tharu woman might have a tattoo of a lion or a tiger to protect her from evil. Bracelets on her wrist are a sign she is married.

The hair of Tharu children, as well as the children of other ethnic groups, is sometimes slick with mustard oil. This makes it easier to comb. A newborn baby is also rubbed with mustard oil because the oil is believed to be good for the child's health.

The Terai, with its tigers and leopards, rhinoceroses, crocodiles, and elephants, is the area of Nepal with the most wildlife. But the wildlife has paid a price for the changes made in the Terai. Entire forests were destroyed to open up land for farming, and many animals were left without homes.

The zebu and the yak are two of Nepal's most useful animals. Zebus are a kind of cattle that farmers use to pull plows or wagons. Yaks are large, shaggy animals related to the cow and the buffalo. They live high in the Himalayas, the mountain range that separates Nepal from Tibet. These hardy animals are often used to carry heavy loads through rugged mountain country. Yaks are also raised for their meat and their milk, and for their hair, which can be made into yarn or cloth.

Nepal's most famous animal may not even exist. According to legend, the Himalayas are home to a mysterious apelike creature called the yeti or abominable snowman. Many people claim to have seen this furry animal, but until its existence can be proven, it will remain a mystery.

To many of the Nepalese, the Himalayas are more than just mountains; they are also said to be the home of the gods. These rugged peaks can be as dangerous as they are beautiful. Climbers risk floods, blizzards, landslides, and earthquakes.

The most famous of the Himalaya Mountains is Mount Everest, the world's tallest mountain. For years people tried, and failed, to climb this peak, which is more than five miles high. Finally, in 1953, New Zealander Sir Edmund Hillary and his Nepalese guide Tenzing Norgay made it to the top.

Norgay was a member of the Sherpa ethnic group. Sherpas live in the mountains and are used to traveling over the steep Himalayan slopes. Since Norgay's successful climb, many Sherpas have given up farming and raising yaks to become mountaineers for at least part of the year. Trekking, or walking the mountain paths, through the Himalayas has become very popular. Tourists often hire Sherpas to act as their guides and to carry their supplies.

It is evening in Nepal. Togendra has sold all of his coconuts and is on his way home with the money he has earned. Rameshoweri and her sister have returned home from Bhaktapur, and their parents have come in from the fields.

The color of the Himalayas begins to change with the setting of the sun. Blue turns to red and then fades to gray in the twilight. In the valley, dim electric lights and oil lamps are lit for a short time before they too are extinguished and the small Himalayan country sleeps.

More about Nepal

What is the capital of Nepal?
The capital of Nepal is Kathmandu.

How many people live in Nepal?
Nepal is home to nearly 20 million people.

How big is Nepal?
The area of Nepal is 56,827 square miles, which is about the size of the state of Illinois.

What is the highest point in Nepal?
Mount Everest is the highest point in Nepal—and in the world. It is 29,028 feet (more than five miles) tall.

What is Nepal's official language?
The official language of Nepal is Nepali, but most of Nepal's ethnic groups have their own languages.

What is Nepal's basic unit of money?
The basic unit of money in Nepal is the *rupee*.

Pronunciation Guide

Bhairab VHY-ruhb

Bhaktapur VHUCK-tuh-puor

Bodhnath Stupa BOHD-nahth STOO-puh

Brahma BRAH-muh

Ganesh GUH-dnaysh

hasia HUHN-see-uh

Kathmandu kaht-mahn-DOO

Lumbini loom-BEE-nee

Newar nay-WAHR

Nyatapola nyuh-TUH-poh-luh

Pashupatinath puh-SHOO-puh-tee-NAHTH

patuka puh-TOO-kah

saranghi SAH-ruhn-gee

Sherpa SHARE-pah

Shiva SHEE-vuh

Siddhartha Gautama sihd-HAHR-thuh GOW-tuh-muh

Skanda skahn-DUH

Swayambunath swuh-YUHM-BOO-nahth

Tamang tah-MAHNG

Terai tuh-RYE

thangka THAHNG-kah

Tharu THAH-roo

topi TOH-pee

Vishnu VIHSH-noo

Index